Loc
State Government

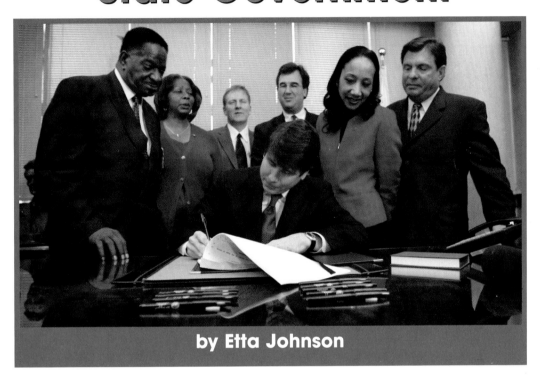

by Etta Johnson

Table of Contents

☆Introduction☆

You follow rules every day. Your family has rules.

Your school has rules. Your teacher makes rules for the classroom.

You follow laws every day, too. The government makes the laws. The government makes sure we follow the laws. Read this book to find out more about the government.

See the Glossary on page 22.

What Is Government?

First, think about your school. Think about the rules. You come to school to learn. Some rules keep you safe. Some rules help you learn.

This student did not follow the rules. What will happen to the student? Adults at school will decide. Adults at school make the rules.

Now think about your **community**. Your community is your town or city. Think about the laws in your community.

Some laws keep you safe. Some laws help you do things.

Your community has people who make the laws. They are part of the government.

Your community has people who make sure the laws are followed. They are part of government.

Dellview
Population: 16

The town of Dellview, North Carolina, is one of the smallest communities in the United States. Fewer than twenty people live there!

What Is Local Government?

Your community has a local government. Most communities have a **mayor**.

Is your community a town?

Is your community a city?

Citizens elect the mayor.

The citizens **elect** the mayor of the community. Citizens are people who have rights in the community where they live. The citizens also elect the **representatives** of the community.

▲ Citizens elect the community representatives.

The mayor and the representatives lead the local government. The local government makes laws.

Judges make sure people follow laws. Judges solve problems about laws. Judges are part of local government.

Did You Know?

How does the governme pay for schools, parks, public health, and other services? State and loca governments collect tax from taxpayers. This ta money is used to pay f government services.

The local government has other jobs. It makes sure the community is safe and clean. It makes sure people have what they need.

Local Government Services

fire stations

trash collection

police

public parks

libraries

schools

What Is State Government?

The government in your state is called the state government.

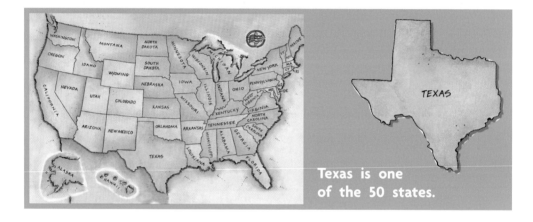

Texas is one of the 50 states.

The state government takes care of the whole state. The leader of the state government is called the **governor**.

The state representatives are part of the state government. They represent the citizens who elect them.

State representatives have meetings. They make decisions about laws.

Judges are part of the state government. Judges make sure people follow the laws. Judges also solve problems about laws.

Then and Now

From 1885 until 1925, Florida used a book to choose the chief justice of its Supreme Court. One at a time, each Supreme Court justice would open the same book. Which justice got to be the chief justice? The one who opened to a page where the first word started with a letter closest to the letter z!

Now, the justice who is chief justice changes every two years. The justices take turns, based on who has been in the court the longest.

What Are the Three Branches of State Government?

State government has three parts. These parts are called "branches."

executive branch

legislative branch

judicial branch

The **executive branch** of government helps to make laws. Citizens elect the governor.

▲ Arnold Schwarzenegger becomes governor of California.

16

▲ **The governor of Mississippi lives here.**

People to Know

The first African American elected as governor in the United States was L. Douglas Wilder. He was governor of Virginia from 1990 to 1994.

The **legislative branch** of state government makes laws.

▼ **Florida's legislative branch meets in Tallahassee.**

Solve This

Number of Senators

State	Senators
Alaska	20
California	40
Florida	40
Illinois	59
Michigan	38
Minnesota	67
New York	62
Texas	31

Senators are part of a state's legislative branch. Which of these states has the most senators in the state legislative branch? Which has the fewest state senators in the legislative branch? What is the difference in number of senators between those two states?

Answers: Minnesota has the most with 67. (Of all 50 states, Minnesota has the most senators in its legislative branch.) Alaska has the least with 20. (Of all 50 states, Alaska has the fewest senators in its legislative branch.) The difference is 47.

The **judicial branch** of government solves problems about laws. Judges work in courts of law to solve the problems. The state government has three branches.

▲ Judges help to solve problems here in Arizona's state courts.

Your community has a local government. Your state has a state government.

Stat

Executive Branch

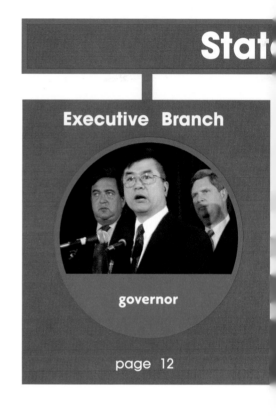

governor

page 12

Local Government

mayor	**local representatives**	**judges**

page 8	page 9	page 10

overnment

Legislative Branch

state
representatives

page 13

Judicial Branch

judges

page 14

Think About It

1. What does your mayor do?
2. What does your governor do?
3. What does a representative do?
4. What does a judge do?

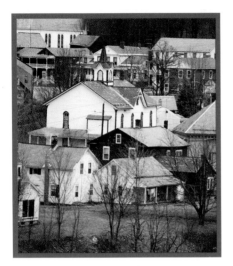

community the town or city where people live and work

*Our **community** is a town.*

elect choose a person for a government job

*Citizens **elect** representatives.*

executive branch part of government that helps make laws

*The governor is the leader of the **executive branch**.*

governor the leader of state government

*Our **governor** is a strong leader.*

judicial branch part of government that solves problems about laws

*Judges work in the **judicial branch**.*

legislative branch part of government that makes laws

*The **legislative branch** works to make laws.*

mayor the leader of local government

*The **mayor** said our city needs more parks.*

representatives people who represent the citizens who elect them

*Our **representatives** have meetings with the people.*